THIS KALIMBA BOOK
BLONG TO :

_____

PHONE NUMBER:

_____

EMAIL:

_____

Hello, we wish you success on your Kalimba learning journey. This book contains 50 Songs. With the number system, you can play songs without having to know musical notes. All songs are arranged to be played easily with the 17-key kalimba in the C setting. If you listen to the track you want to play beforehand, you can learn the songs much easier and faster. Make sure the tuning of your kalimba is correct before starting to work.

SONGS

1. A Whole New World
2. Animal Crossing
3. Arirang
4. Ashokan Farwell
5. Avatar : The Last Airbender
6. Bella Ciao
7. Colors Of The Wind
8. Pirates Of Caribbean (Davy Jones)
9. Dirty Old Town
10. Feliz Navidad
11. Für Elise
12. Game of Thrones Main Theme
13. Green Green Grass Of Home
14. Happy Birthday Song
15. Pirates Of Caribbean (He's A Pirate)
16. Happy New Year
17. Heart & Soul
18. Hedwig's Harry Potter
19. Hedwig's Harry Potter (Hard)
20. House Of The Rising Sun
21. I's The B'y
22. Indiana Jones (Raiders March)
23. Jack And Jill
24. Jingle Bell Rock
25. Jurasic Park Main Theme
26. Kalimba Lullaby
27. Let It Snow
28. Lukey's Boat
29. Wiegenlied Lullaby
30. La La Land
31. Mononoke Hime
32. My Bonnie Lies Over The Ocean
33. Our House
34. Planxty Irwin
35. Pokemon Center
36. Pussy Cat , Where Have You Been ?
37. Rocky Top
38. Silent Night
39. Star Wars Main Theme
40. The Canadian Minuet
41. The Linden Tree
42. Traumerei
43. Waltzing Matilda
44. We Wish You A Marry Christmas
45. La Vie En Rose
46. Believer (Imagine Dragons)
47. Melody of The Night
48. Merry Go Round Of Life
49. Moonlight Densetsu - Sailor Moon
50. Test Drive

A Whole New World

SANTA KALIMBA

Aladdin OST

Animal Crossing

SANTA KALIMBA

6 4 2 1 6 4   2 5   4 5 6 2 3 4 1

6 4 2 1 6 4   2 5   4 5 6 2 3 4 1   6 4 2 1 6 4 2

5

Arirang

SANTA KALIMBA

Korean Folk Song

♩ = 100

5 6 5 6   1 2 1 2   3 2 3 1 6   5 6 5   1 2 1 2

3 2 1 6 5 6   1 2 1   1   5 5   5 3 2   3 2 3 1 6

5 6 5   1 2 1 2   3 2 1 6 5 6   1 2 1   1

3

Ashokan Farwell

SANTA KALIMBA

Jay Ungar

Avatar's Love
Avatar: The Last Airbender

Jeremy Zuckerman

BELLA CIAO

SANTA KALIMBA

Traditional

3 6 7 1 6   3 6 7 1 6   3 6 7 1 7 6 1   1 7 6 3 3 3

2 2 3 4 4 4   4 3 2 3 3 3   2 2 1 7 3 1   1 7 6

3 5 7 1 6   3 6 1 7 6   3 6 7 1 6 6 1   1 7 6 3 3 3

2 2 3 4 4 4   4 3 2 3 3 3   2 2 1 7 3 1   1 7 6

6

Colors of the Wind

SANTA KALIMBA

Alan Menken & Stephen Schwarts

Davy Jones Theme
Pirates of the Carribean

SANTA KALIMBA

Hans Zimmer

8

Dirty Old Town

SANTA KALIMBA

♩ = 160

5 6 1   3   2 1 3 1   5   3 5   6   5 3 2 1

3   3   6 5   3   3 2 1 3 1   5   6 1 3   2

2   2 1 6   6

9

Feliz Navidad

SANTA KALIMBA

5   1 7 1   6   6   2   1   6   5   5   1   7   1

6   4 6   6 5   5   5   5   5   4   4   3   3   3   3   3   3   2 1

1   6   6   6   2 2   2   2   1   6   6   5   5   5   3   3   3   3   2 1

1   6   6   6   2 1   7   7   1   2   1   1

FÜR ELİSE

SANTA KALIMBA

Ludwig van Beethoven (1770-1827)

11

Game of Thrones Main Theme

SANTA KALIMBA

Ramin Djawadi

Green Green Grass of Home

SANTA KALIMBA

Curly Putnam

HAPPY BIRTDAY SONG

SANTA KALIMBA

He's A Pirate
Pirates of the Caribbean

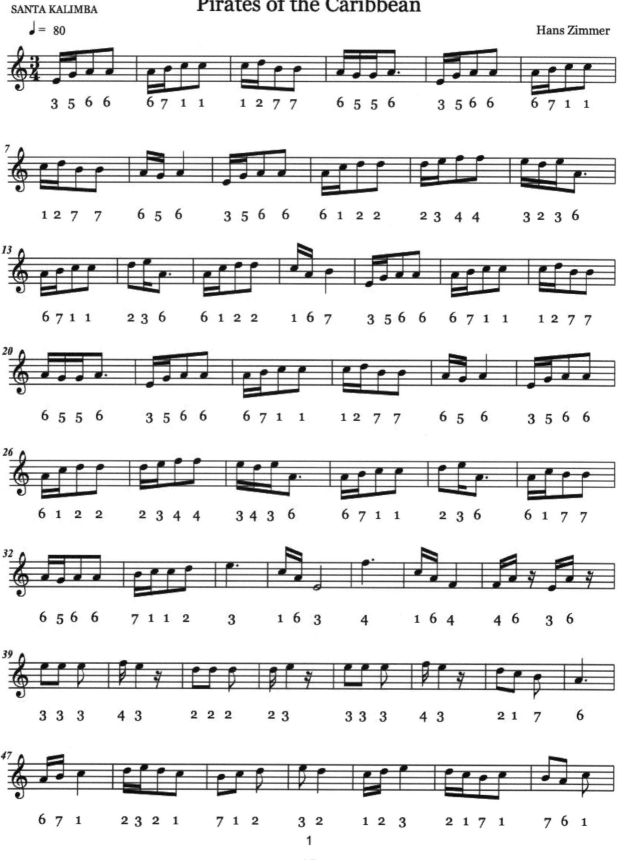

SANTA KALIMBA

Hans Zimmer

15

Happy New Year

SANTA KALIMBA

Heart & Soul

SANTA KALIMBA

Arr. Thoma'Nimation

1 1   1   1 1 7 6   7 1 2   3 3   3   3 3 2 1

2 3 4   5   1   1 6 5 4   3 2   1 1 7   6 7 6 5

4 5 4 3   2 5   1 1   1   1 1 7 6   7 1 2   3 3

3   3 3 2 1   2 3 4   5   1   1 6 5 4   3 2   1 1 7

1 7 6 5   4 5 4 3   2   5

18

Hedwig's
Harry Potter

SANTA KALIMBA

John Williams

Hedwig's
Harry Potter (Hard)

John Williams

SANTA KALIMBA

♩ = 140

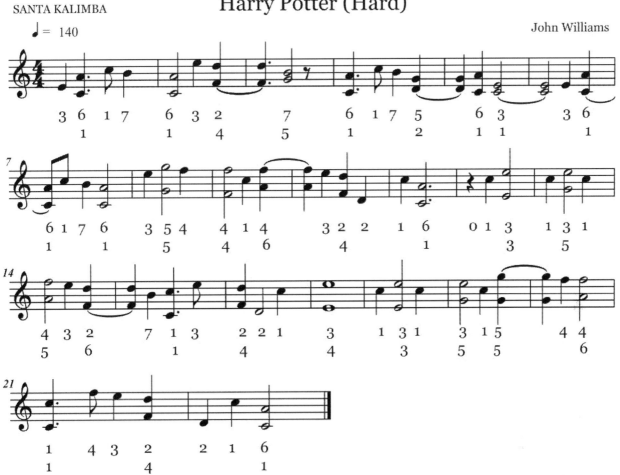

House of the Rising Sun

SANTA KALIMBA

3   6 7 1 3   2 6 6 6   6 6 5 3   3   6 6

6   7 1   3   2 6   6 6 6 6   6   6 6 5   2 5   6

21

I's The B'y

SANTA KALIMBA

Newfoundland folk song

6 6 6 6   5 5 3 1 1   6 6 6 6   7 1   6 6 6 6

5 5 3 1 1   1 1 3 5 3   4 4   6 6 6 6   5 3 1 1

6 6 6 6   7 7 1   6 6 6 6 6   5 3 1 1   1 3 5 3

4   4

Indiana Jones
(Raiders March)

SANTA KALIMBA

John Williams

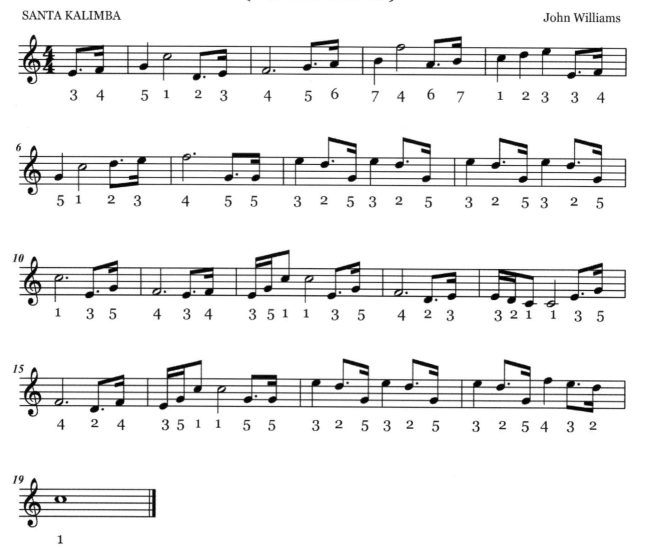

Jack and Jill

♩ = 140

| 6 | 6 | 6 | 6 | | 2 | 2 | 2 | 2 | | 3 | 3 | 3 | 3 | | 4 | 2 | | 6 | 6 | 6 | 6 |
| 4 | 4 | 4 | 4 | | 4 | 4 | 4 | 4 | | 5 | 5 | 5 | 5 | | 6 | 4 | | 4 | 4 | 4 | 4 |

| 7 | 7 | 7 | 7 | | 6 | 5 | 4 | 3 | | 2 | 2 |
| 5 | 5 | 5 | 5 | | 4 | 3 | 2 | 1 | | | |

Jingle Bell Rock

SANTA KALIMBA

Robby Helms

Jurasic Park
Main Theme

SANTA KALIMBA

John Williams

Kalimba Lullaby

SANTA KALIMBA

ILHAN OZCAN

1 3 2 1 1   2 4 3 2 2   3 5 4 3 3   2 1 7 1 1

1 2 3 4 5   1 7 1 2 2   7 1   3 3 4 3 2 1   1   5 5 5

6 5 3 2 1   1 2 1 7 6   6 5 4 3 2 1   1 3 5 1

7 5 6 7 1   3 3 2 1 1   3 3 2 1 1   2 2 3 2 1 1

7 7 7 1 3   2 2 3 2 1 1   7 6 5 7 1

27

Let It Snow, Let It Snow, Let It Snow

SANTA KALIMBA

Jule Styne

Lukey's Boat

Canadian folk song

SANTA KALIMBA

1   4 5 6 1   4 5 6 2   1   2   1   1   4 5 6 1

4 5 6 4   5 3 1 5   6 4 1 1   4 4 5 5 3   4

Lullaby - Wiegenlied

SANTA KALIMBA

Johannes Brahms

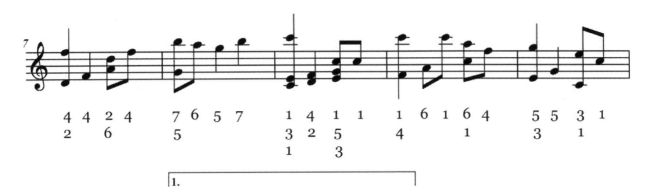

Mia & Sebastian's Theme

La La Land

SANTA KALIMBA

Mononoke Hime
Princess Mononoke

Joe Hisaishi

My Bonnie Lies Over the Ocean

SANTA KALIMBA

Traditional

Our House

Planxty Irwin

SANTA KALIMBA

Traditional

Pokemon Center

SANTA KALIMBA

Junichi Masuda

1 5 1 5 4 3   2 7   7 5 7 3 2 7   1 3   1 5 1 5 4 3

2 7   7 5 7 3 2 7   1   3 5   4 5 4 3 2   7 2

3 4 3 2 1   3 5   4 3 4 5 6   5 4 3 4   3 4 3 2 1

Pussy Cat, Pussy Cat, Where Have You Been?

SANTA KALIMBA

♩ = 100

1 4 4 4 3 4   5 6 4 5   2 3 4 5 6 7   1 1 6 4

1 4 4 4 3 4   5 6 4 5   2 3 4 5 6 7   1 1 6 4

Rocky Top

SANTA KALIMBA

Silent Night

SANTA KALIMBA

5 6 5   3   5 6 5   3   2 2   7   1 1   5   6 6

1 7 6   5 6 5   3   2 2   4 2 7   1   3   1 5 3

5   4   2   1

Star Wars Main Theme

SANTA KALIMBA

John Williams

40

The Canadian Minuet

SANTA KALIMBA

6 6 6 6 6   6 3 1   1 1 1 1 1   1 6 1   3 3 3 3 3

1.   2.

3 4 5 3   6 3 1 6 1 2   3 3 2 1   3 3 2 1   1 1 1 1 1

1 5 4 3 2 1   2 2 2 2 2   2 4 3 2 1 7   6 1 6 1 3

6 5 6 3 2 1   4 2 1 7 6 5   6

The Linden Tree

TRAUMEREI

SANTA KALIMBA   ROBERT SCHUMANN

43

Waltzing Matilda

SANTA KALIMBA

We Wish You A Merry Christmas

SANTA KALIMBA

♩ = 100

5

1 1 2 1 7   6 6 6   2 2 3 2 1   7 5 5
3   5   4   3   2   4   5   4

3 3 4 3 2   1 6   5 5   6 2 7   1   1 5
3   7   6   3   4   2   3
                                                    5

45

La Vie En Rose

Édith Piaf

Believer
Imagine Dragons

4

51

Melody of the Night No. 5

SANTA KALIMBA

Shi Jin

Merry Go Round of Life
Howl's Moving Castle

SANTA KALIMBA

Joe Hisaishi

1

Moonlight Densetsu
SAILOR MOON

SANTA KALIMBA

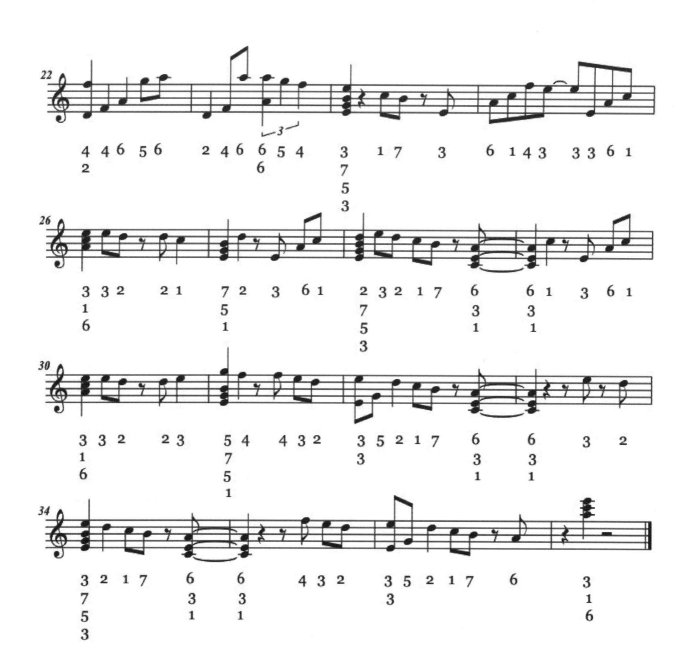

Test Drive

John Powell

Made in United States
Orlando, FL
21 November 2024